Foreword

by Christine Bulmer

Ever since I married a cider-maker over forty years ago I have used the family product for cooking in a variety of ways.

We have frequent visitors to the house — we are a large family — and my husband has always liked to bring his business friends home to a meal. We find that our guests particularly appreciate the discovery of the range and versatility of this drink.

People often ask me why I don't publish some of my recipes, but as I cook largely by guesswork I would be hard put to it to write down anything that would be of use to anyone else.

Consequently, I was delighted to talk to Mary Berry about her book and to find that she has worked out the quantities and ingredients of the recipes and presented them in such a way that they will be a certain success. I hope that readers will enjoy them.

It is difficult to have enough variety in our everyday meals, and here is an opportunity of finding out, by following Mary Berry's suggestions, how much a little cider can add interest to your cooking.

Christine Bulmer

D1482413

Contents

3 **Foreword**

5 **An introduction to cider**

15 **Spring**
16 Bishop's Creamed Chicken
17 Clementine Beef
18 Lamb Boulangère
20 Cornish Ham Pie
21 Caramelised Bananas
22 Mustard Glazed Collar of Bacon
24 Cider Malt Loaf
25 Austrian Locksmith's Apprentice
26 Handsome Maud's Special Trifle
28 Syllabub

29 **Summer**
30 Herrings in Cider
32 Italian Chicken
34 Creamed Paprika Pork
36 Mild Curried Chicken
37 Tarragon Chicken
38 Fresh Fruit Salad
40 Coronation Peaches
41 Summer Meat Loaf
42 Crunchy Cider Cake
44 Mackerel with Gooseberry Sauce

45 **Autumn**
46 Moules Marinières
48 Poacher's Pigeon Casserole
49 Treacly Chops
50 Bodior Pie
52 King's Pyon Pork Chops

53 Chicken Trala
54 Jugged Hare
56 Pears in Woodpecker
57 Apple Posset
58 American Cider Sherbet
60 Salter's Meadow Teabread

61 **Winter**
62 Pork and Tomato Casserole
64 Winter Vegetable Casserole
66 Herefordshire Red Cabbage
68 Liver Hotpot
69 Tatter's Pie
70 Saturday Fish Pie
72 Swiss Steak
73 Fondue
74 Mincemeat
76 A First-Rate Plum Pudding
78 Herefordshire Cider Cake

79 **Cider for drinking**
82 Chairman's Special
84 Pomagne Cocktail
85 Midsummer Fruit Cup
86 Henley Special
87 Iced Grapefruit
87 Fresh Summer Sparkler
88 Summer Celebration Cup
89 Hereford Redstreak
90 All Seasons Fruit Cup
92 Sangria
93 Blackcurrant Cooler
94 Glühwein
96 Champion's Cup
96 Orange Quencher

Mary Berry's cider recipes & drinks

CIDER FOR ALL SEASONS

Published in association with
H P Bulmer Limited
by Woodhead-Faulkner Limited
7 Rose Crescent, Cambridge CB2 3LL

Woodhead-Faulkner Ltd
7 Rose Crescent, Cambridge CB2 3LL

First published 1977
© H. P. Bulmer Limited 1977
ISBN 0 85941 036 6

Conditions of sale
All rights reserved. No part of this publication may be reproduced,
stored in a retrieval system or transmitted, in any form or by any
means, electronic, mechanical, photocopying, recording or otherwise, without the prior permission of the copyright owner.

Photography by Bryce Attwell

Tiles from World's End Tiles & Flooring Ltd, 9 Langton Street,
London SW10.

China, kitchenware and ovenware from Harrods, Knightsbridge,
London SW1; Elizabeth David, 46 Bourne Street, London SW1;
David Mellor, Sloane Square, London SW1; Peter Jones, Sloane
Square, London SW1; Habitat, King's Road, London SW3.

Cover design and text layout by Ken Vail.

Production services by Book Production Consultants.
Typesetting by Amos Typesetters Ltd.

Printed and bound in Great Britain by William Clowes & Sons Ltd,
Beccles, Suffolk.

An Introduction to Cider

Stay me with flagons, comfort me with apples,
For I am sick of love. SONG OF SOLOMON

The apple is a remarkable fruit. At various times, it has been worshipped or vilified, looked upon as sacred or treated with contempt. It was an instrument of man's temptation by woman, yet deified by the Celts. An apple a day, so it is said, keeps the doctor away and teachers, traditionally, are bribable with apples.

Cider, of course, is quite another matter. "It is indeed bad to eat apples. It is better to make them all into cider", said a North American Indian to a missionary after hearing the story of Adam and Eve. Such primitive wisdom is merely another example of an attitude stretching back thousands of years. The ancient Britons tasted the apples growing wild in the forests of southern Britain and found them bitter. But pressed to a pulp and

the juice left to ferment, those same apples produced a drink that fortified the Celts, sent them strong-armed into battle, consoled their defeats and celebrated their victories.

For centuries, cider and ale have been the drinks of the countryman. Britain is the home of the great apple orchards, with isolated areas of Kent and East Anglia growing apples on a large scale. The farmers of Herefordshire, Gloucestershire, Somerset and Devon grew apples for their own use, extracting the juice by means of traditional presses, using wild yeasts to aid fermentation and storing it in oak casks. What they and their families could not drink themselves would be sold locally.

Cider-making by these primitive means produced unpredictable fermentation and the quality of the cider varied considerably from farmhouse to farmhouse.

Cider was an acceptable drink for young and old, rich and poor, pious and impious. The abbeys and priories in apple-growing areas were quick to exploit the commercial properties of cider and largely contributed to the growing popularity of cider in the Middle Ages. Many a well-covered friar rolled cheerily into Vespers after quaffing flagons of home-brewed cider, and many a traveller recovered his spirits after a journey with cider from the same source.

The Church became quite concerned at the lay population's attitude to cider, roundly condemning the widespread practice of baptising infants in it.

Cider drinking received a boost during the Hundred Years War. The aristocracy, who by and large preferred to drink wine, regarding cider as the property of lesser mortals, found that their supplies of wine were cut off by the inconvenient and drawn-out war with France. In desperation they turned to the home-based product and discovered, to their delight, that cider possessed qualities they had never suspected. Many confirmed wine-drinkers never touched the grape again.

Cider was a popular drink in Tudor and Elizabethan times. All sorts of methods were used to improve the quality of the brew. Legs of mutton were placed in vats of fermenting apple juice to add to the natural nutrients and help the growth of yeast, and sulphur candles were burned to sweeten the barrels. But as long as cider-making remained a cottage industry, its quality was a very hit-and-miss affair.

Hundreds of different varieties of cider apples were grown as farmers experimented with their orchards to see what characteristics the resulting cider possessed. The names of these apples reflect the personalities of the men who created them and have contributed to the romantic picture of cider-making and drinking that many people have today. Some are lyrical, some humorous, some earthy. What rustic wag, for example, christened an apple Slack-my-Girdle or Sheep's Nose? Then there are Bloody Butcher, Foxwhelp, Lady's Finger and Cat's Heads. Ruby Streak and Golden Ball need no further description. Perhaps it was a lovesick, apple-growing swain who chose Handsome Maud's as the name of his new creation.

In the seventeenth century, there were no fewer than 350 named varieties weighing down the cider-apple trees of England. Some of these trees grew in the Herefordshire orchards of the 1st Viscount Scudamore, who tired of the trivialities of court life in the reign of King Charles I and returned to his estate. Here, he set about selecting the variety known as Red Streak, the most famous seventeenth-century apple of all. It was due to his interest and patronage that cider drinking reached a peak of popularity at this period. Noble palates throughout the country learned to discern subtle differences in cider blends and, as their sophistication grew, so did the skill of the cider makers in producing beverages pleasing to all tastes.

It was the first Golden Age of cider and, as a tribute to Lord Scudamore, Herefordshire was dubbed "the orchard of all England". But the Golden Age did not last. As the eighteenth century developed and industrialisation began to alter the landscape, people caught up in the rigours of the new era found oblivion to the hardships easier to achieve with gin. At the other end of the social scale, improvements to roads and coach travel brought Continental touring back into vogue and wine replaced cider on the rich man's table. Cider drinking returned to its pastoral image.

The doldrums for cider lasted for over one hundred years, until a West Country Member of Parliament, Radcliffe Cooke, turned the promotion of cider drinking into a personal crusade. At every opportunity he would leap to his feet in the House of Commons and exhort his fellow Members to support the sagging cider industry. His colleagues treated his efforts as a bit of a joke, calling him the "Member for Cider", but the general public took his exhortations to heart, sampled the "golden beverage" and decided they liked it. Once again, cider joined the best-seller league.

The Victorian Golden Age was shorter-lived than its predecessor two centuries earlier. But it heralded the first large-scale production of cider, and companies that are now household names in cider-making came into being. One of the reasons was scientific. The wild yeasts that caused unpredictable fermentation in the ciders produced in cottage and farmhouse had made it impossible to guarantee the quality of the cider on sale. But Bulmers, founded in Hereford in 1888, managed to isolate a yeast that dominated fermentation. Cider of guaranteed quality could now be manufactured in quantities calculated to satisfy a wide range of tastes.

Public drinking habits, however, are notoriously fickle. The general view of cider was picturesque and poetic rather than sophisticated, so that although sales grew slowly in the early years of this century cider was more a drink associated with walking tours in the rustic peace of the West Country than one favoured by the frenzied cocktail party set of the Twenties.

Nevertheless, cider production was on the increase. But, welcome though this was to the cider manufacturers, a major problem now marred the outlook. The problem was apples, or rather the lack of them. For more than a thousand years, apple-growing had kept pace with cider-making. Suddenly, it looked as though the demand for cider would outstrip the yield of cider apples. The traditional orchards of forty large trees to the acre were simply not producing enough fruit.

The cider manufacturers began to look for ways in which they could help the growers to increase production. One scheme was to start a nursery so that growers could be supplied with young trees at low cost. The density of orchards was examined, together with methods of improving growing conditions and collecting the harvest. In the last seventy years, research stations have been set up, looking into such things as disease resistance and heavier cropping. One result of this work is that bush trees have taken the place of large trees in modern orchards, making it possible to grow anything from 160 to 600 trees to an acre. Side by side with the development of more intensive farming methods has been the technological advance in turning the fruit into a drink.

Today, cider-drinking is entering a third Golden Age. Six centuries ago, it was the war in France which made cider popular. Now, one of the reasons is the high duty levied on imported wines. But credit must also go to cider-makers who have endeavoured to offer a wide range of ciders to suit all occasions.

How Cider is made

Apples are the fruits of autumn, that season of mists and mellow fruitfulness. For the cider-maker, the period between early October and late November represents the busiest time of the year, as thousands upon thousands of tons of apples begin to arrive at the cider factories.

The apples come in four categories, each containing many different varieties. The categories are designated according to the amount of acid and tannin contained in the apple. It is these two components which determine the flavour of the cider and their ratio to each other is as important as their quantity.

Sweet apples are those which are low in both acid and tannin, producing a very bland cider, used mainly for blending with very strong ciders.

Bittersweet apples have a low acid content but are high in tannin. Their cider is both astringent and bitter, although these flavours can vary considerably in degree. Characteristic English cider is made from bittersweet apples.

Sharp apples are exceptionally high in acid, exceptionally low in tannin. Their flavour is similar to the cooking apple, which is sometimes used instead of the true sharp cider variety.

Bittersharp, the fourth category of apple used, was once the most popular class of apple for cider-making. Compared with the other categories, it is high in acid and tannin, but the range of its flavours is not as great as that of the bittersweet.

The harvesting of cider apples has always been a quicker task than gathering culinary and dessert apples. Cider apples are hard and do not bruise easily but the odd bruise or two has little effect on the final product, and the traditional method of harvesting the apples, by giving the tree a good shake so that the ripe fruit falls to the ground, can be followed.

In the past, the fruit had to be picked up and bagged by hand. Today there are machines to cope with that job, although some of the smaller farms still employ apple-pickers to scoop the apples into hand-held bags. The most popular machine in the large orchards is one which shakes the tree and catches the falling fruit in a cloth frame. It is, however, extremely difficult to manoeuvre, especially among high-density orchards. Another ingenious machine operates rather like a lawn-mower, with revolving blades that sweep the apples off the ground into the machine where they are winnowed before being passed to a container.

On its arrival at the factory, the fruit is tipped into huge concrete silos, where all the bits of grass, twigs and other debris are washed away by water. A rotary drum gives the apples a final wash and they then pass to the vital crushing stage.

First the apples are broken up and beaten to a pulp in a mill containing serrated knives, and collected in a hopper. From this, the pulp moves to the press, which consists of a series of pulp-filled cloths sandwiched between slatted wooden boards. The layers of cloths are known as "hairs" or a "cheese". Using hydraulic pressure, the "cheese" is squeezed until the juice runs out to be collected in settling vats.

In recent years, new methods of extracting the juice from the pulp have been developed. In one, the pulp is pumped into a cylinder containing a hydraulically operated piston which compresses the pulp and forces the juice out. The cylinder can be rotated and the same pulp pressed time and time again until no more juice can be extracted. The cylinder is then emptied and the process is repeated with a fresh batch of pulp.

Another method of collection is by means of a machine called the screw press, which enables a continuous supply of juice to be extracted. As the screw turns, it forces the pulp down the cylinder, squeezing harder and harder until all the juice has been forced out. Used pulp is extracted at the bottom as new pulp is being put in at the top.

The next stage in cider-making is the most important. This is the process of fermentation which takes from three to four weeks. During this time yeast is added which turns the sugar in the juice to alcohol. The fermentation vats were traditionally made of wood, but today concrete or mild steel vats lined with acid-resistant resins are used.

When fermentation has finished, the result is a very dry cider, which after racking and fining is now considered suitable for storage. The extreme dryness prevents bacteria from forming which could give the cider an "off" flavour. It also allows the cider to remain in good condition for twelve months or more.

This, of course, is very important, since apple-pressing can take place only once a year. But the manufacturers must be able to supply cider the whole year round and must be able to store several million gallons at any one time. At one time, 100-gallon oak casks were used for storage. At the turn of the century, bigger vats were built in seasoned English oak, capable of holding up to 60,000 gallons. But the First World War affected cider-making just as it affected every other walk of life. In 1919, when seasoned oak was in short supply, glass-lined concrete rectangular tanks were designed, each with a capacity of 100,000 gallons.

These tanks sound huge, but they were Lilliputian compared with the storage vats of today. In 1954 a 45-foot-high steel tank was built to hold half a million gallons. But the biggest tank of all — the largest container for alcoholic drink in the world — holds 1,650,000 gallons and was built in 1975. Following a tradition of giving each storage tank a name, it was called Strongbow.

When cider was made on tiny presses in farms and

cottages, the left-over pulp, known as pomace, was never wasted but was used to feed the livestock on the farm. Modern cider-makers are just as thrifty as their forebears but more commercially minded.

Pomace, for example, contains pectin, which every housewife knows is the gelling agent vital to successful jam-making. Pectin is extracted from the pomace, concentrated and sold in liquid or powder form.

After the pectin has been removed, the residue is dried, fortified with nutrients and turned into cattle feed.

Keeping Cider

Although cider does not need the long maturing process required by wine, maturation is very important as it turns the fermented apple juice into true cider. Blending and sweetening to give each cider its particular flavour takes place just before marketing. The variety of ciders available is described in the drinks section at the end of the book, but for most people new to cider drinking the problem is not so much which cider to choose but how to store the many different varieties when you have them.

Traditional draught cider is sold only to public houses and requires a knowledgeable cellarman to keep it in peak condition. This is because it has a small amount of yeast added to it before it is put in casks, which sets up a secondary fermentation, and it must therefore be stored at a constant temperature if it is not to deteriorate.

Most ciders are sold in large bottles and cans, and may be still or sparkling. The sparkling varieties have had carbon dioxide injected into them and, like any other fizzy drink, will go flat in time once they are opened. Unopened cider, however, will last up to two years provided it is kept in a reasonably cool temperature, say 45°–50°F (8°–10°C). Pomagne, sparkling cider, on the other hand, should not be kept longer than eighteen months unopened, as it can be affected by air in the headspace.

Bottles of cider which have been opened should be stored in the refrigerator. Cider goes flat less quickly if it is chilled and will still be quite drinkable after two days. If you are merely using it for cooking, however, it will last about two weeks. Remember, in cooking, it is the flavour of the cider that is important, not the effervescence.

Cider for Cooking

One of the big advantages of cider in the kitchen is that there is no such thing as a "cooking" cider. All cider is sold for drinking. The fact that it improves so many cooked dishes is a happy accident and means that no drop need ever be wasted. What you don't need for a particular recipe can be drunk later, either in between meals or with them.

Cider adds a fruitiness to cooked dishes which in some recipes, particularly those with a base of apples or pears, is invaluable. It goes very well with all white meats, such as chicken or pork, improves fish and lifts an ordinary dish into the gourmet class. In sweet dishes, it adds body to recipes which might otherwise be somewhat bland, and has a mellowing effect on some cake recipes. In fact, in many dishes where a quantity of liquid is required, cider can be used for all or as part of the liquid to good effect.

A new Golden Age for cider is in progress at the moment. It has been called the Great Cider Revival and refers to cider as a beverage. But for the discerning housewife, it should become the Great Cider Cooking Revival as well.

Spring-Apple Blossom Time

Strong heart; full English courage
Out of Hereford soil
Sweet and strong, the pride of Englishmen.
SUSAN BROWN 1967

Spring is the season when the apple orchards clothe themselves in glory, the season of promise and hope. But it is also the time when the weather is unpredictable and chill winds and sudden frosts can nip our fingers and button up our coats. Springtime meals need variety; they must be warm and comforting on cold days, light and refreshing when summer really is only just round the corner. This is where cider is so versatile. It adds body to dishes that sustain us and gives a welcome kick to recipes with a light touch. Use it to improve the quality of stews and sauces.

Bishop's Creamed Chicken

for four

An interesting combination that goes well with a mixture of peas and rice.

4 chicken joints
1½ oz (40 g) flour
2 oz (50 g) butter
1 onion, chopped
¾ pint (450 ml) dry cider such as Dry Reserve
2 tablespoons (30 ml) lemon juice
1 bayleaf
Salt and pepper
6 oz (175 g) packet frozen sweetcorn
Parsley to garnish

Toss the chicken joints in the flour. Melt the butter in a large frying pan and fry the chicken until a golden brown. Remove and place on one side.

Add the onion to the fat remaining in the pan and cook gently for 5 minutes. Stir in the remaining flour and cook for 2 minutes. Add the cider and lemon juice and bring to the boil, stirring. Season and add the bayleaf. Return the chicken joints to the pan; cover and simmer for about 25 minutes.

Add the sweetcorn and cook for a further 10 minutes or until the chicken is tender. Adjust the seasoning if necessary. Turn into a serving dish and serve garnished with parsley.

Clementine Beef

for four

The cider and orange in this recipe gives an extra special flavour to this stew.

2 onions
2 carrots
1½ lb (700 g) stewing steak
1½ oz (40 g) plain flour
1½ oz (40 g) dripping
1 large orange
¼ pint (150 ml) dry cider such as Strongbow
About ¼ pint (150 ml) water
1 beef stock cube
Salt and pepper

Peel and chop the onions, then peel and slice the carrots. Cut the meat into 1-inch cubes and coat in the flour.

Melt the dripping in a saucepan, then add the meat and fry quickly to brown. Stir in any remaining flour and add the onions and carrots.

Peel rind thinly from the orange and cut into thin strips. Squeeze the juice from the orange and add to the cider; make up to ¾ pint (450 ml) with water.

Add the rind and liquid to the pan with the beef stock cube and seasoning; bring to the boil. Cover and simmer for 1½ to 2 hours or until tender.

Lamb Boulangère

for six to eight

This is a perfect dish for, say, a supper in the kitchen with friends; serve straight from the oven. No need for extra vegetables, just crisp French bread for those who are extra hungry.

3½ lb (1½ kg) boned shoulder of lamb
½ lb (225 g) pork sausagemeat
Grated rind and juice of half a lemon
1 rounded tablespoon (30 ml) freshly chopped parsley
Salt and pepper
1½ lb (700 g) potatoes
½ lb (225 g) onions
½ pint (300 ml) dry cider such as Strongbow
A little chopped parsley

Heat the oven to 350°F (180°C), Mark 4.

Trim any excess fat from the lamb. Mix the sausagemeat, parsley, seasoning and the rind and juice of the lemon and spread over the lamb. Roll up and tie securely.

Peel the potatoes and cut into thick slices. Peel and slice the onions and mix with the potatoes; lay in an ovenproof dish and season well. Put the lamb on top and pour over the cider. Cover with a piece of foil and roast for 30 minutes to the lb and 30 minutes over. After the first hour remove the foil and baste the meat and potatoes.

When cooked, sprinkle the potatoes and onions with a little chopped parsley and serve straight from the oven.

From top to bottom:
Clementine Beef, Cornish Ham Pie, Lamb Boulangère

Cornish Ham Pie

for six

A good way of using the last cuts of a ham or bacon joint.

1½ oz (40 g) butter
1½ oz (40 g) flour
¼ pint (150 ml) milk
¼ pint (150 ml) medium-dry cider such as Dry Woodpecker
8 oz (225 g) cooked ham or bacon
2 hard-boiled eggs, chopped
1 rounded tablespoon (30 ml) chopped parsley
Salt and pepper
1 large 13 oz (368 g) packet puff pastry

Heat the oven to 425°F (220°C), Mark 7.

Melt the butter in a saucepan, add the flour and cook for 2 minutes. Add the milk and cider and bring to the boil, stirring. Simmer for 2 to 3 minutes until thickened.

Cut the ham into neat ¼-inch dice and add to the sauce with the eggs and parsley. Mix well, season to taste and leave to cool.

Cut the pastry in half and roll out each piece to a circle 10 inches in diameter. Place one piece on a baking sheet and spread over the filling, leaving a border at the edge. Damp the edge with milk or water and cover with the remaining piece of pastry, firmly sealing the edges. Cut any trimming into leaves and use to decorate the top of the pie.

Brush with milk and bake in the oven for 20 to 25 minutes until well risen and golden brown. Transfer to a serving dish and serve with a green vegetable such as beans and whole baked tomatoes.

Caramelised Bananas

for four

Serve at once with plenty of thick cream.

8 bananas
2 oz (50 g) butter
¼ pint (150 ml) Apple Juice
2 oz (50 g) demerara sugar

Peel and slice the bananas. Melt the butter in a large frying pan and fry the bananas until slightly coloured. Add the Apple Juice and sugar and boil rapidly until thick and treacly.

Serve at once with cream.

Mustard Glazed Collar of Bacon

for eight

Collar of bacon cooked in Apple Juice has a lovely flavour. If required, the Apple Juice may be thickened with a little cornflour to make a sauce.

3 lb (1½ kg) collar of bacon
1 pint (600 ml) Apple Juice
1 onion, thinly sliced
Freshly ground black pepper
3 oz (75 g) demerara sugar
1 level tablespoon (15 ml) dry mustard

Soak the collar in cold water for 12 hours or overnight. Drain and place in a saucepan. Pour over the Apple Juice, adding a little more if necessary to make sure that the joint is just covered. Add the onion and pepper; cover and bring to the boil. Simmer for 1¼ hours or 20 minutes to the lb plus 20 minutes over.

Remove the joint from the saucepan and leave to cool slightly. Remove the skin and score the fat diagonally into diamond shapes; stand the collar in an ovenproof dish.

Mix together the sugar and mustard and pat into the surface of the bacon. Cover the lean meat with a piece of foil and brown the joint in a hot oven, 425°F (220°C), Mark 7, for about 15 minutes to give a rich golden glaze.

Cider Malt Loaf

A very quick loaf to make, best eaten on the day it is made.

6 oz (175 g) self-raising flour
1 level tablespoon (15 ml) malt drink (Ovaltine)
1 oz (25 g) caster sugar
3 oz (75 g) mixed dried fruit
2 level tablespoons (30 ml) golden syrup
⅓ pint (189 ml) sweet cider such as Woodpecker

Place all the ingredients together in a bowl and mix to a thick batter. Put into a greased 1-lb loaf tin and bake in the centre of the oven, 325°F (170°C), Mark 3, for about 1 hour or until cooked through in the centre.

Leave to cool in the tin and serve sliced with butter.

Austrian Locksmith's Apprentice

makes sixteen and serves four

A crisp confection best served with lightly whipped cream for dessert.

16 large prunes
16 blanched almonds
2 oz (50 g) flour
5 tablespoons (75 ml) sweet cider such as Woodpecker
Deep fat for frying
1 oz (25 g) grated chocolate
1 oz (25 g) caster sugar

Soak the prunes overnight. Carefully remove the stones from each prune and in its place put an almond.

Place flour in a small bowl and stir in the cider; mix well to make a thick batter. Heat the fat for frying, coat each prune in the batter and drop into the fat. Fry over a moderate heat for about 3 minutes until crisp and golden brown, remove and drain on kitchen paper.

Mix the chocolate and sugar together and roll the hot prunes in the mixture until each is lightly coated. Serve warm with whipped cream.

Handsome Maud's Special Trifle

for six

Why Handsome Maud? You may well ask! This is the name of one of the 350 varieties of cider apple that have been used through the ages. This trifle is an old-fashioned one and deliciously potent.

6 individual sponge cakes, split in half
Raspberry jam
8 oz (225 g) raspberries
2 oz (50 g) ratafia biscuits
8 tablespoons (120 ml) Dry Reserve cider
2 tablespoons (30 ml) Calvados
3 egg yolks
1 oz (25 g) caster sugar
1 heaped teaspoon (10 ml) cornflour
½ pint (300 ml) milk
¼ pint (150 ml) double cream
½ oz (12½ g) almonds, blanched, split and lightly toasted

Sandwich the sponge cake halves together with the jam and arrange with the raspberries on the bottom of a shallow 2-pint (1¼-litre) serving dish.

Top with the ratafia biscuits and pour over the cider and Calvados.

Mix together the egg yolks, sugar and cornflour. Warm the milk in a saucepan over a low heat until it is hand-hot and pour it on to the yolks, stirring constantly. Return the mixture to the saucepan and cook gently, stirring until it thickens. Do not allow to boil or the custard will curdle. Allow to cool, then pour over the sponge cakes and leave to set.

Whisk the cream until it is thick and spread it over the custard. Decorate with almonds.

From top to bottom:
Handsome Maud's Special Trifle, Syllabub

Syllabub

for six

Syllabub today is a far cry from the syllabub of Elizabethan times, when the cow was milked straight into a bucket containing cider or wine and the resulting frothy liquid was sweetened and served as syllabub. I prefer today's rich, more firm confection.

Half a lemon
¼ pint (150 ml) sweet cider such as Woodpecker
1 tablespoon (15 ml) brandy
2 oz (50 g) caster sugar
¾ pint (450 ml) double cream

Finely grate the lemon rind and squeeze out the juice. Put the rind and juice in a bowl with the cider, brandy and sugar, and stir until the sugar has dissolved.

Pour in the cream and whisk until the mixture will form soft peaks when the whisk is lifted out.

Spoon into six individual glasses and leave in a cool place until required. Serve with cat's tongues or boudoir biscuits.

Summer-Season of Plenty

*A kind of cider, made of a fruit
of that country, a wonderful pleasing
and refreshing drink.*   FRANCIS BACON 1561–1626

When you are hot and tired there is no more refreshing
drink than cider. It is indeed the best of all summer
drinks, a cool drink with a sparkle that restores you to
life. But it is also a fine addition to summer recipes. Fruit
salads take on a special quality when laced with cider.
Ham baked in cider is a special treat at a summer picnic.
Fish dishes are uplifted when served with a sauce to
which cider has been added. It is the ideal ingredient in
all recipes planned for long summer days.

Herrings in Cider

for four

Choose very fresh large herrings. A lovely inexpensive dish to make.

4 herrings
Salt and pepper
1 small onion, finely chopped
1 apple, finely chopped
1 level tablespoon (15 ml) chopped parsley
Butter
½ pint (300 ml) dry cider such as Strongbow

Remove the bones from the herrings, clean and lay flat. The fishmonger will always do this for you if asked.

Season the inside of the fish with salt and pepper. Mix the onion, apple and parsley together and spread over the herrings. Roll up.

Butter an ovenproof dish and lay the fish in it. Pour the cider around them and bake in the oven, 350°F (180°C), Mark 4, for about 40 minutes. Serve the herrings with cider spooned over them.

Italian Chicken

for six

This is a colourful dish and full of flavour.

3½ lb (1½ kg) chicken
½ pint (300 ml) extra-dry cider such as Bulmers Number 7
2 onions, chopped
Black pepper
Salt
Milk
2 oz (50 g) butter
2 oz (50 g) flour
1 canned red pepper, drained and sliced

Put the chicken and giblets in a small roasting tin or casserole. Add the cider and onions and season with black pepper and salt. Cover with foil or a lid and cook at 350°F (180°C), Mark 4, for 20 minutes to the lb and 20 minutes over, *i.e.* about 1½ hours. Test to see if it is cooked by piercing the thick part of the leg with a skewer; if the juices come out clear the bird is done. If the juices are bloody continue cooking until they are clear. Lift the chicken out to cool and strain off the remaining liquid in the tin. Skim off the fat and make up to 1¼ pints with milk.

Save the liver with the chicken, remove the meat from the chicken, cutting it into good-sized pieces. Chop the liver. Use the carcass and giblets to make stock for soup on another occasion.

Melt the butter in a saucepan, add the flour and cook for 2 minutes. Stir in the stock and milk. Bring to the boil, stirring, and allow to thicken. Add the red pepper and season with lots of black pepper and salt.

Stir in the meat and allow to become piping hot. Turn into a serving dish.

Creamed Paprika Pork

for four

A great favourite of mine for entertaining. It waits
happily in the oven — 275°F (140°C), Mark 1 — for half
an hour or so and then the cream is added at the very last
moment. Serve with buttered noodles or rice and
broccoli.

1¼ lb (550 g) pork fillet
2 tablespoons (30 ml) salad oil
1 oz (25 g) butter
1 onion, chopped
1 level tablespoon (15 ml) paprika pepper
1 level tablespoon (15 ml) flour
¼ pint (150 ml) stock
¼ pint (150 ml) medium-dry cider such as Dry Woodpecker
5 tablespoons (75 ml) sherry
1 level teaspoon (5 ml) tomato purée
Salt and pepper
6 oz (175 g) small button mushrooms
¼ pint (150 ml) soured cream
chopped parsley

Cut the pork into 1½-inch pieces. Heat the oil in a pan, add the butter and then fry the pork pieces quickly until they are just beginning to brown. Remove from the pan and drain on kitchen paper.

Add onion and paprika to the pan and fry for 2 minutes. Blend in the flour and cook for a further minute. Remove from heat and stir in the stock, cider and sherry. Return to the heat and simmer until thick. Add tomato purée and seasoning to the meat; cover and simmer for 30 to 40 minutes or until the pork is tender.

Wash the mushrooms and add to the pan, cover and simmer for 5 minutes.

Just before serving, blend in the soured cream and check seasoning. Turn the pork on to a serving dish and, if liked, garnish with triangles of fried bread and chopped parsley.

From top to bottom:
Creamed Paprika Pork, Italian Chicken, Mild Curried Chicken

Mild Curried Chicken

for six

Cider when added to a curry takes away any sharpness and the result is mellow and full of flavour. As a drink cider goes so well with any curry, especially when well chilled.

6 chicken roasting joints
1½ oz (40 g) flour
1½ level teaspoons (7½ ml) salt
1 large onion
2 oz (50 g) butter or margarine
3 level teaspoons (15 ml) hot curry powder
1 level tablespoon (15 ml) paprika pepper
½ pint (300 ml) medium-dry cider such as Dry Woodpecker
2 dried red chillies
1 level tablespoon (15 ml) mango chutney
1 teaspoon (5 ml) Worcester sauce
1 lb (400 g) can pineapple cubes
2 bayleaves

Remove skin from chicken joints. Toss in the flour and salt. Finely chop the onion.

Melt the butter in a pan and fry the chicken quickly to brown, remove and keep on one side. Add the onion to the pan and fry for 5 minutes until soft. Stir in the curry powder, paprika pepper and remaining flour; fry for 2 minutes. Return the chicken to the pan with the remaining ingredients including the pineapple syrup. Cover the pan and simmer gently on the top of the cooker for 45 minutes or until tender. Alternatively cook in the oven, 325°F (170°C), Mark 3, for about 1 hour.

Remove the bayleaves and chillies before serving.

Tarragon Chicken

for four

For the instant chef! Five minutes to prepare, 45 minutes to cook. If you don't like chicken skin pull off the skin first. If you do not have fresh tarragon use fresh chives. For special occasions add 2 tablespoons of cream to the sauce just before serving. Serve with boiled rice.

One 1 pint (600 ml) packet chicken or celery soup
1 onion, finely grated
1 tablespoon (15 ml) freshly chopped tarragon
½ pint (300 ml) dry cider such as Strongbow
4 chicken joints
Freshly ground black pepper

Heat the oven to 350°F (180°C), Mark 4.

Mix the packet of soup, onion, tarragon and cider together in a casserole and drop in the chicken joints. Season with black pepper and bake covered in the oven for 45 minutes or until the chicken is tender. Check seasoning before serving.

Fresh Fruit Salad

for six

It is essential to leave the fruit salad marinading overnight for the flavour to blend. Serve very cold.

4 oz (100 g) granulated sugar
¼ pint (150 ml) extra-dry cider such as Bulmers Number 7
Juice of half a lemon and strips of lemon peel
2 oranges
1 grapefruit
3 pears
2 apples
½ lb (225 g) black or white grapes
2 bananas

Dissolve the sugar over a low heat in the cider with the lemon juice and strips of peel. Strain into a bowl and leave to cool.

Peel the oranges and grapefruit and cut into segments; add to the syrup.

Peel, core and slice the pears and apples. Stir into the syrup so that they are thoroughly coated in the syrup to prevent discoloration.

Pip the grapes and skin if liked and add to the fruit. Cover the bowl and leave in a cool place overnight to marinade.

Just before serving, peel and slice the bananas and mix in with the rest of the fruit. Turn into a serving dish and serve with plenty of cream.

From top to bottom:
Fresh Fruit Salad, Coronation Peaches

Coronation Peaches

for six

When peaches are at the height of their season and inexpensive this is a lovely dessert to make. Don't make it more than 6 hours ahead of the meal, or otherwise the peaches will discolour. Make sure that all the peaches are immersed in the liquid or the exposed part will go brown. Spoon out into old-fashioned pudding bowls or deepish dishes as the juice is the best part; you will need a spoon and fork to tackle the whole peach.

4 oz (100 g) granulated sugar
¼ pint (150 ml) water
6 ripe peaches
½ pint (300 ml) sweet cider such as Woodpecker
3 tablespoons (45 ml) brandy (optional)

Dissolve the sugar in the water in a pan over a low heat and cool.

Put the peaches in a basin and cover with boiling water. Leave for a minute, then turn all the peaches at once into a bowl of cold water and remove the skins by gently peeling them off. Prick each peach with a stainless steel fork right through to the stone in several places. As each peach is peeled and pricked put them into a glass bowl just big enough to take the six. Cover with first the sugar syrup, then ¼ pint cider, and finally the brandy so that the peaches are immersed completely. Cover with a plate and chill for 6 hours. Also chill the remaining ¼ pint cider.

Just before serving, stir in the remaining cider which will make the peach juice fizzle and sparkle. Serve with cream very cold.

Summer Meat Loaf

for six

Adding liver to this meat loaf makes it extra moist. It is a very good Saturday lunch dish if you have guests for the weekend — and it does not cost the earth to make.

½ small onion
6 oz (175 g) pig's liver
8 oz (225 g) pork sausagemeat
8 oz (225 g) best mince
1 rounded tablespoon (30 ml) chopped mixed fresh herbs
1 level teaspoon (5 ml) salt
½ level teaspoon (2.5 ml) pepper
4 tablespoons (60 ml) dry cider such as Dry Reserve
Garnish:
1 tomato
A little chopped parsley

Heat the oven to 350°F (180°C), Mark 4.

Peel the onion and cut in half and put through the mincer with the pig's liver. Place in a large bowl with the remaining ingredients and mix very thoroughly.

Press the mixture firmly into a 1-lb loaf tin, measuring about 6½ inches by 4 inches across the top. Stand the tin in a dish of hot water in the centre of the oven and bake for 1¼ hours. Leave to cool in the tin; chill.

Turn out on to a serving dish and garnish with tomato slices and a thin line of chopped parsley down the centre.

Serve sliced with a green salad.

Crunchy Cider Cake

This is a real family cake best eaten on the day that it is made. You can even eat it with whipped cream as a pudding.

8 oz (225 g) self-raising flour
1 level teaspoon (5 ml) baking powder
3 oz (75 g) butter
3 oz (75 g) caster sugar
Grated rind of a lemon
1 egg
¼ pint sweet cider such as Woodpecker
For the topping:
1 oz (25 g) self-raising flour
2 oz (50 g) soft brown sugar
1 oz (25 g) butter, melted

Heat the oven to 375°F (190°C), Mark 5. Grease and line the base of an 8-inch loose-bottomed cake tin.

Sift together the flour and baking powder. Add the butter, cut into small pieces and rub into the mixture. Stir in the sugar and lemon rind. Lightly beat the egg and add, with the cider, to the mixture, stirring well until blended. Turn into the cake tin.

Mix the flour and sugar for the topping in a basin; add the melted butter and mix with a fork until crumbly. Sprinkle over the cake.

Bake for about 40 minutes until cake is risen and golden brown. Leave to cool in the tin for 5 minutes before turning out, then leave on a wire rack until cold.

Mackerel with Gooseberry Sauce

for four

Mackerel is an inexpensive fish and when served with this tart gooseberry sauce makes a delicious supper dish.

¾ lb (325 g) gooseberries
¼ pint (150 ml) sweet cider such as Woodpecker
1 rounded tablespoon (30 ml) cornflour
1 tablespoon (15 ml) cold water
1 tablespoon (15 ml) sugar or to taste
4 small or 2 large mackerel, filleted
Seasoned flour
2 oz (50 g) butter
Juice of half a lemon
A little chopped parsley

Wash the gooseberries, place in a pan with the cider, and stew gently until tender and sieve. Put the cornflour and the water in the saucepan and blend, stir in the gooseberry purée and return to the heat. Bring to the boil, stirring continuously, and allow to thicken. Simmer for 2 to 3 minutes before adding the sugar, still stirring.

Dip the mackerel fillets in the flour. Melt the butter in a frying pan and fry the fish for about 6 to 8 minutes, turning once. Place on a warm serving dish. Add the lemon juice and parsley to the pan and heat through. Pour over the fish and serve with the gooseberry sauce.

Autumn–The Fruits of Harvest

Lo! For thee my mill
Now grinds choice apples
And British vats o'erflow
With generous cider.   JOHN PHILIPS 17th century

Autumn is the busiest time of the year for the growers of apples and the makers of cider. But this is no reason to make it a time of hard work for the cook. It is here that cider displays its greatest advantages. It gives a special flavour to dishes which might otherwise be dull — even the humble apple pie takes on a fruitiness, when cider is added, which is hard to beat. Even the pastry can be made with cider. The clocks go back one hour in the autumn, but the traditions of cider drinking and of using cider in cooking go back centuries.

Moules Marinières

for four

When buying mussels allow 1½ pints per person. Take care not to overcook them — they take only a few minutes, just until the shells open.

6 pints (3½ litres) fresh mussels
1 oz (25 g) butter
4 shallots
4 parsley stalks
2 sprigs fresh thyme *or* ¼ level teaspoon dried thyme
1 bayleaf
Freshly ground black pepper
½ pint (300 ml) dry cider such as Strongbow
Salt
Chopped parsley
For the beurre manié:
1 oz (25 g) soft butter
½ oz (12½ g) flour

Scrape and clean each mussel with a strong knife, removing every trace of seaweed, mud and beard. Wash in several changes of water, discarding any badly chipped or cracked ones that do not close tightly. Mussels which remain open are dead and should not be used. Drain the mussels in a colander.

Melt the butter in a large pan over a low heat. Peel and chop the shallots, add to the pan and fry until they are soft but not brown. Add herbs, pepper, cider and mussels to the pan. Cover with a tight-fitting lid and cook quickly, shaking the pan constantly until the mussels are open (about 5 to 6 minutes). Lift the mussels out, discard the empty half of the shell and keep hot in a covered dish. Reduce the liquor to about ½ pint (300 ml). Remove the fresh thyme, parsley stalks and bayleaf.

Blend the flour and butter for the *beurre manié* to a smooth paste. Drop the *beurre manié* into the simmering stock a teaspoon at a time and whisk it until the stock is smooth and has thickened. Add more pepper and salt if necessary. Pour the stock over the mussels and scatter with plenty of chopped parsley.

Serve with French bread and butter.

Poacher's Pigeon Casserole

for four

Other game birds such as pheasant and grouse may also be cooked in this way.

4 pigeons
3 tablespoons (45 ml) oil
½ lb peeled button onions
1 rounded tablespoon (30 ml) flour
¾ pint (450 ml) dry cider such as Strongbow
Grated rind and juice of half an orange
1 tablespoon (15 ml) redcurrant jelly
½ lb (225 g) chestnuts, peeled and skinned
Salt and pepper
Chopped parsley

Heat the oven to 350°F (180°C), Mark 4.

Cut each pigeon in half along the breastbone and trim off the backbone and wings to leave just the breast and thick part of the leg.

Heat the oil in a large pan and fry the pigeons and onions in the oil for 3 to 4 minutes until brown. Transfer to a large 4½-pint casserole.

Stir the flour into the oil remaining in the pan and cook for 1 minute. Add the cider, orange rind and juice and redcurrant jelly, and bring to the boil, stirring. Simmer for 2 minutes to thicken and pour over the pigeons.

Add the chestnuts and seasoning to the casserole. Cover and cook in the oven until the pigeons are tender (about 1 hour but this can vary with the age of the pigeon).

Serve sprinkled with chopped parsley.

Treacly Chops

for four

Quick to make, this dish will cook happily whilst the vegetables are cooking. Nice served with plain boiled potatoes and broccoli.

4 good-sized pork chops
Salt and pepper
A little butter
½ pint (300 ml) Apple Juice
1 level tablespoon (45 ml) freshly chopped sage *or*
¼ level teaspoon dried sage

Trim the surplus fat from the chops and season well.

Rub a frying pan with a little butter and fry the chops on both sides until almost done (about 10 minutes). Drain off any excess fat in the pan, add the Apple Juice and sage, and simmer for 5 minutes. Lift out the chops and place on a serving dish. Boil the Apple Juice rapidly until a thick treacly sauce is obtained; pour over the chops and serve.

If you like a lot of sauce don't reduce the Apple Juice — just thicken with a little cornflour.

Bodior Pie

for four to six

A really delicious pie, made for me by Mrs Bertram Bulmer. Ever since, I might say, I have been making it frequently for my family. It makes a perfect dish for family lunch or an informal party. Make it ahead and all you need to serve with Bodior pie is a green salad and hot crunchy bread. Heat the bread in the oven with the pie for the last five minutes or so.

1 lb (450 g) piece of collar or bacon hock
About ¾ pint (450 ml) medium-dry cider such as Dry
    Woodpecker
1 lb (450 g) potatoes
2 oz (50 g) butter
2 oz (50 g) flour
½ pint (300 ml) milk
6 oz (175 g) mushrooms, sliced
3 hard-boiled eggs, roughly chopped
Salt and pepper
2 oz (50 g) Cheddar cheese, grated
1 oz (25 g) Parmesan cheese, grated

Place the bacon in a pan and add just enough cider to
cover. Cover the pan with a lid and simmer gently for
about 20 minutes or until cooked.

Meanwhile boil the potatoes in their skins until cooked,
drain, peel and slice.

Remove the bacon from the pan and cut into neat cubes.
Boil the cider rapidly until it is reduced to ½ pint
(300 ml).

Melt the butter in a large saucepan, add the flour and
cook for 2 minutes. Stir in the milk and cider and bring to
the boil, stirring. Add the mushrooms and simmer for 5
minutes. Add the bacon, potato and eggs; mix well and
season to taste. Turn into a 3½-pint (2-litre) ovenproof
dish and sprinkle with the cheese. Place under a medium
grill until golden brown and hot through. If the pie has
been made in advance put in a fairly hot oven, 375°F
(190°C), Mark 5, for 20 to 25 minutes.

Serve with French bread and a green salad.

From left to right:
Bodior Pie, King's Pyon Pork Chops, Chicken Trala

King's Pyon Pork Chops

for six

A special way of serving pork chops. Well worth trying when mushrooms are plentiful in the fields.

6 pork chops
Salt and pepper
8 oz (225 g) button mushrooms
2 oz (50 g) butter
1½ oz (40 g) flour
½ pint (300 ml) dry cider such as Dry Reserve
1 teaspoon (5 ml) fresh chopped herbs *or* good pinch dried
  mixed herbs
5 oz (150 ml) carton soured cream *or*
5 oz (150 ml) carton double cream soured with a teaspoon
  lemon juice
Chopped parsley

Remove the rack from the grill pan and line the pan with a piece of foil. Lay the chops on this and season well with salt and pepper. Grill chops for about 15 minutes, turning once, or until they are crisp and brown. Transfer the chops to a serving dish and keep hot. Reserve the juices on the foil.

Fry the mushrooms gently in the butter for 2 minutes. Remove them from the pan. Stir the flour into the butter and cook, stirring for 1 minute. Gradually add the cider, stirring constantly. Blend in reserved meat juices and herbs and bring to the boil, stirring. Return the mushrooms to the sauce and simmer for 3 to 4 minutes, stirring constantly or until the sauce has thickened. Check seasoning.

Add cream and heat gently. Do not allow to boil. Serve with the sauce poured over the chops. Scatter with fresh chopped parsley.

Chicken Trala

for six

Chicken goes so well with cider and there are many chicken recipes which include it. Chicken Trala is special, easy and very rich. Choose simple vegetables to go with it such as creamed potatoes and courgettes.

3½ lb (1½ kg) chicken
1 bottle Bulmers Number 7
Salt and pepper
Milk
¾ lb (325 g) onions
2 oz (50 g) butter
1½ oz (40 g) flour
2 level teaspoons (10 ml) curry powder
¼ pint (150 ml) soured cream

Put the chicken in a small roasting tin or casserole, with the giblets and cider. Season well and cover with a tight-fitting lid or piece of foil. Cook in the oven, 350°F (180°C), Mark 4, for about 1 hour 10 minutes or 20 minutes to the lb. Remove from the oven and leave to cool overnight in the casserole.

Remove the chicken from the stock and carve into thin slices. Heat the stock gently, strain into a measure and make up to ¾ pint (450 ml) with milk.

Slice the onions finely. Melt the butter in a pan, add the onions, cover and cook gently until soft but not brown (about 10 to 15 minutes).

Stir in the flour and curry powder and cook for 2 minutes. Add the stock and milk and bring to the boil, stirring.

Add the chicken and heat through. Adjust the seasoning and, just before serving, stir in the soured cream.

Jugged Hare

for six to eight

A dry cider is a natural for jugged hare.

1 small hare, cut into neat pieces
2 oz (50 g) bacon fat
2 large onions, chopped
1 stick celery, chopped
Salt and pepper
1 bayleaf
Grated rind of half a lemon
1 pint (600 ml) medium-dry cider such as Dry Woodpecker
¼ pint (150 ml) water
1 rounded tablespoon (30 ml) redcurrant jelly
1 oz (25 g) butter
1 oz (25 g) flour

Fry the hare joints in the bacon fat in a large pan until browned. Put into a large ovenproof casserole with the vegetables, salt and pepper, bayleaf and lemon rind. Pour over the cider and water and cover the casserole with a tight-fitting lid. Put it in the oven, 325°F (170°C), Mark 3, for about 2½ to 3 hours or until the hare is tender.

Remove the hare and place on a warm serving dish. Strain the gravy into a pan and add the redcurrant jelly. Stir until dissolved.

Cream the butter in a small bowl and work in the flour to make a smooth paste. Add, in small pieces, to the gravy, whisking until smooth. When all the butter has been added to the gravy, bring to the boil and simmer until it has thickened. Adjust the seasoning if necessary. Pour over the hare and serve with forcemeat balls and fried croûtons.

Pears in Woodpecker

for four

Pears cooked in cider have a wonderful flavour. Serve them with whipped cream.

1½ lb (700 g) cooking pears
4 oz (100 g) granulated sugar
4 cloves
½ pint (300 ml) sweet cider such as Woodpecker
A little cochineal to colour

Peel, quarter and core the pears and place in a saucepan with the sugar, cloves and cider. Add a little pink colouring, cover and simmer gently until the pears are tender (about 45 minutes).

Remove the cloves and serve the pears either hot or cold with whipped cream.

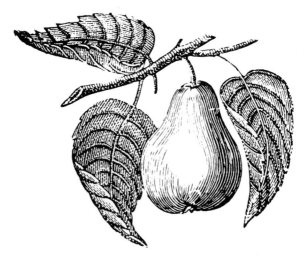

Apple Posset

for four

Such a good way of serving apples. The cider and cinnamon give it a special flavour.

1½ lb (700 g) cooking apples
½ pint (300 ml) sweet cider such as Woodpecker
Sugar to sweeten
¼ level teaspoon cinnamon
1 rounded tablespoon (30 ml) cornflour
A little whipped cream
Browned halved almonds

Peel, core and roughly slice the apples. Place in a pan with the cider, sugar to taste and cinnamon. Cover and cook slowly until very soft. Sieve or put through the blender until a smooth purée.

Mix the cornflour to a smooth paste with a little extra cider or water in the saucepan. Add the apple purée and bring slowly to the boil, stirring. Simmer for 2 minutes.

Remove from the heat and leave to cool slightly. Turn into a glass serving dish or individual glasses and chill.

Just before serving, spread the top with a little cream and decorate with browned almonds.

American Cider Sherbet

for twelve

This is a very good way of using up windfall apples.

1½ lb (700 g) apples, peeled, cored and sliced
6 oz (175 g) granulated sugar
1 tablespoon (15 ml) lemon juice
½ oz (15 g) gelatine
3 tablespoons (45 ml) cold water
½ pint (300 ml) sweet cider such as Woodpecker

Turn the freezer to its lowest setting.

Place the prepared apples in a pan with the sugar and lemon juice. Cover and cook slowly, stirring occasionally until soft. Sieve or beat to form a smooth purée. Leave to cool.

Place the gelatine in a small bowl or cup with the cold water and leave to stand for 3 minutes to become a sponge. Place in a small pan of simmering water and leave until dissolved and clear. Cool slightly.

Mix together the gelatine, apple purée and cider, then turn into a rigid container and leave until almost set in the freezer.

Turn into a large bowl and whisk until light and fluffy. Return to the container and freeze until solid.

Remove from freezer and leave to stand at room temperature for 10 minutes before serving.

Salter's Meadow Teabread

To my mind there is no need to butter this teabread. It is a marvellous recipe — no scales needed. Soak all but the flour and egg overnight, then add them to the other ingredients and bake. Beautifully moist and easy to cut, it is so popular in our house at the moment that I am making one a fortnight. Keeps very well if allowed to!

1 breakfast cup (½ pint, 300 ml) currants
1 breakfast cup (½ pint, 300 ml) sultanas
1 breakfast cup (½ pint, 300 ml) brown sugar
1 breakfast cup (½ pint, 300 ml) sweet cider such as
    Woodpecker
1 egg
2 breakfast cups (1 pint, 600 ml) self-raising flour

Put the fruit, sugar and cider in a bowl and stir well. Cover and leave to stand overnight.

Heat the oven to 325°F (170°C), Mark 3. Grease and line an 8-inch round cake tin.

Stir the egg and flour into the fruit mixture and mix thoroughly. Turn into the cake tin and bake in the oven for 1½ hours. Leave to cool on a wire rack and serve either sliced with butter or just as it is.

Winter-Rosy Cheeks & Christmas Cheer

Yes, alone this British beverage
Cider, built and fortified man,
Ingrained the Bulldog courage
Whether sailor, soldier or yeoman.   ANON 17th century

Cooking with cider is particularly appetising in winter.
The strong apple flavour gives a lift to all sorts of winter
dishes and, because the acids in cider counteract the fats
in the food, even rich meals are more digestible.
Christmas recipes are specially suited to cider. Mincemeat is more tasty and plum pudding has more body.
And when the main dish is very filling, cider added to the
starter makes an appetising and piquant introduction to
the meal. Cider is a fine addition to puddings, especially
the hot puddings which all the family enjoy on cold
winter days.

Pork & Tomato Casserole

for four

Pork and cider are naturals. This is an especially good casserole which looks after itself with no last-minute things to do.

1 oz (25 g) butter
4 pork chops
2 small onions
4 sticks celery
14 oz (397 g) can peeled tomatoes
Salt and pepper
¼ pint (150 ml) medium-dry cider such as Dry Woodpecker

Melt the butter in a frying pan and fry the chops until golden brown on both sides.

Peel and very finely slice the onions and celery. Put in a bowl with the tomatoes and seasoning and mix well. Place half the mixture in a casserole, lay the chops on top and spoon over the remaining mixture. Pour over the cider.

Cover the casserole and bake in the centre of a moderate oven, 350°F (180°C), Mark 4, for about 1 hour or until the chops are tender.

Winter Vegetable Casserole

for four to six

Try variations on this theme according to the vegetables in season. Be sure not to overcook the vegetables so that they still have a slight bite in the centre.

½ pint (300 ml) medium-dry cider such as Dry Woodpecker
½ pint (300 ml) water
8 oz (225 g) carrots, peeled and sliced
½ small cauliflower, broken into flowerets
8 oz (225 g) small sprouts
1 oz (25 g) fresh white breadcrumbs
2 tablespoons (30 ml) salad oil
1 oz (25 g) butter
Salt and pepper
Cheese sauce:
1 oz (25 g) butter
1 oz (25 g) flour
¼ pint (150 ml) milk
1 teaspoon (5 ml) made mustard
4 oz (100 g) grated cheese
Salt and pepper

Bring the cider and water to the boil in a saucepan and add some salt. Put in the carrots and cook for 8 minutes. Add the cauliflower and sprouts and cook for a further 10 minutes or until tender.

While the vegetables are cooking fry the breadcrumbs in the oil and butter, stirring frequently, until they are brown. Season, then remove from the pan and keep hot.

Drain the vegetables, reserving ¼ pint of the vegetable water, and place in a warmed serving dish. Keep hot.

To make the sauce: Melt the butter in a saucepan and stir in the flour. Cook, stirring constantly, for 2 minutes. Remove the pan from the heat and gradually stir in the milk and vegetable water. Return pan to the heat. Bring to the boil and simmer, stirring, for 2 minutes. Stir in mustard, cheese and seasoning.

Pour the sauce over the vegetables, sprinkle with the breadcrumbs and serve at once.

Herefordshire Red Cabbage

for six to eight

A very good and warming vegetable to serve with meat dishes.

1 medium red cabbage
1 lb (450 g) apples, weight after peeling and coring
¼ pint (150 ml) dry cider such as Strongbow
1½ oz (40 g) sugar
1 teaspoon (5 ml) salt
4 cloves
6 tablespoons (90 ml) vinegar
2 oz (50 g) butter
1 tablespoon (15 ml) redcurrant jelly

Trim, clean and finely shred the cabbage. Slice the apples and place with the cabbage in a pan. Add the cider, sugar, salt and cloves. Cover and simmer until tender (about ¾ hour).

Remove the cloves and add the vinegar, butter and redcurrant jelly. Blend well over the heat. Check seasoning and serve hot.

From left to right: Herefordshire Red Cabbage, Winter Vegetable Casserole, Liver Hotpot

Liver Hotpot

for four to five

The secret of this recipe is not to overcook the liver — if you do, it will be tough. Make the sauce ahead and drop the liver in for the last 10 minutes.

½ lb (225 g) onions
2 oz (50 g) dripping
2 oz (50 g) flour
½ pint (300 ml) dry cider such as Strongbow
½ pint (300 ml) water
3 tablespoons (45 ml) tomato ketchup
¼ level teaspoon marjoram
A few drops of Worcester sauce
Salt and pepper
1 lb (450 g) pig's liver

Peel and slice the onions. Melt the dripping in the pan, add the onions and fry for 5 to 10 minutes until the onions are golden brown. Stir in the flour and cook for 2 minutes. Add the cider and water and bring to the boil, stirring until thickened. Add ketchup, marjoram, Worcester sauce and seasoning, mix well and cover the pan. Reduce the heat and simmer gently for about 20 minutes.

Cut the liver into long strips about ½ inch wide. Add to the hot sauce and cook gently for about 10 minutes or until just cooked. Serve at once.

Tatter's Pie

for six

Make sure to use a metal tin for this recipe because you then get a really brown crust underneath. A foil dish would be ideal.

4 oz (100 g) button mushrooms
1½ oz (40 g) butter
1½ oz (40g) flour
½ pint (300 ml) medium-dry cider such as Dry Woodpecker
Pinch mixed dried herbs
Salt and pepper
8 oz (225 g) diced cooked turkey
13 oz (368 g) packet puff pastry

Fry the mushrooms gently in the butter for 2 minutes, remove them from the pan. Stir in the flour and cook, stirring, for 1 minute. Gradually add the cider, stirring constantly. Bring to the boil and simmer for 2 minutes. Add herbs, seasoning, mushrooms and turkey to the sauce. Mix well and leave to cool.

Cut the pastry into two pieces, one slightly bigger than the other, and use to line the base and sides of an 8-inch sandwich tin or pie plate. Put in the turkey mixture and spread flat. Moisten edges of pastry with water. Roll out the remaining pastry to a circle to fit the top and press the edges firmly together with a knife or fork. Roll out the trimmings, cut into leaves and use to decorate the top of the pie. Brush with a little milk and make two slits in the top. Bake in the oven at 425°F (220°C), Mark 7, for 25 to 30 minutes.

Saturday Fish Pie

for four

So called because it is a good dish to make ahead on Friday and reheat and brown on Saturday when it is nice to be with the family rather than slaving over a hot stove!

1 large 14 oz (396 g) packet frozen cod steaks
¼ pint (150 ml) medium-dry cider such as Dry Woodpecker
Milk
1½ oz (40 g) butter
1½ oz (40 g) flour
2 hard-boiled eggs, roughly chopped
1 level tablespoon (15 ml) chopped parsley
1 level tablespoon (15 ml) chopped chives
Salt and pepper
1 lb (450 g) potatoes, cooked and mashed with a little milk
    and butter
1 oz (25 g) cheese, grated

Place the cod steaks in a pan and pour over the cider, cover and poach gently until cooked (about 15 to 20 minutes). Drain the cider into a measure and make up to ½ pint (300 ml) with milk. Flake the fish and put on one side.

Melt the butter in a saucepan and stir in the flour. Cook for 2 minutes. Add the cider and milk mixture to the pan. Bring to the boil, stirring continuously. Cook for 2 more minutes.

Add the flaked fish, eggs, parsley and chives, and mix well. Season to taste. Turn into a well-buttered 2-pint (1¼ litre) ovenproof pie dish.

Top with mashed potato and leave in a cool place until the next day.

Heat the oven to 375°F (190°C), Mark 5. Sprinkle the top of the pie with grated cheese and bake for 30 to 40 minutes until golden brown and hot through.

Swiss Steak

for four

A good winter dish. Serve with buttered noodles and a bright green vegetable.

1½ lb (700 g) chuck steak, cut in one slice 1 inch thick
1 oz (25 g) flour
1 level teaspoon (5 ml) salt
¼ level teaspoon pepper
1½ oz (40 g) lard
3 onions
2 sticks celery
8 oz can (225 g) peeled tomatoes
2 level teaspoons (10 ml) tomato purée
½ teaspoon Worcester sauce
¼ pint (150 ml) dry cider such as Strongbow

Heat the oven to 300°F (150°C), Mark 2.

Cut the steak into 8 pieces. Mix together the flour, salt and pepper. Toss the meat in the flour mixture, pressing it in so that all the flour is used.

Melt the lard in a frying pan, fry the meat quickly on all sides until brown. Transfer it to an ovenproof casserole. Peel and finely slice the onions and slice the celery. Add to the pan and fry in the remaining fat until a pale golden brown. Add to the meat with the tomatoes, purée, Worcester sauce and cider. Cover and cook in the oven for 2½ to 3 hours or until tender.

Fondue

for four

A lovely informal way of entertaining. Serve the fondue in the dish in which it is cooked and keep warm over a spirit lamp or on a hot plate. Heat a French loaf in the oven and cut into 1-inch cubes; serve piled in a dish with the fondue. The guests then take a cube of bread on the end of a fork or skewer and dip it into the fondue.

1 clove garlic, peeled
1 lb (450 g) mature Cheddar cheese
1 pint (600 ml) dry cider such as Strongbow
1 oz (25 g) cornflour
Salt and pepper
1 tablespoon (15 ml) Calvados (optional)

Crush the garlic very finely and grate the cheese. Pour all but about 3 tablespoons of the cider into a thick casserole. Add the garlic and cheese and heat the mixture very slowly until the cheese has dissolved. Do not allow to boil.

Blend the cornflour with the remaining cider in a bowl until smooth. Add a little of the hot cheese mixture to the cornflour and return it to the pan. Carefully bring the fondue to the boil, stirring all the time until the mixture has thickened. Add the salt and pepper, stir in the Calvados and serve at once.

Mincemeat

Makes about 5 lb

Mincemeat made with cider has a lovely rich flavour.

1½ lb (675 g) stoned raisins
½ lb (225 g) cooking apples
4 oz (100 g) candied peel
12 oz (325 g) currants
8 oz (225 g) sultanas
6 oz (175 g) shredded suet
½ level teaspoon mixed spice
2 lemons
1 lb (450 g) soft brown sugar
6 tablespoons (90 ml) extra-dry cider such as
    Bulmers Number 7

Finely chop or mince the raisins and peel. Peel, core and mince or chop the apples. Place in a large bowl with the other fruit, suet and spice.

Grate the rind and squeeze the juice from the lemons. Add to the fruit with the sugar and cider. Mix well.

Cover the bowl and leave to stand overnight. Next day turn into clean jars, cover and label.

A First-Rate Plum Pudding

This old-fashioned rich Christmas pudding improves with keeping. Boil it for at least 10 hours in total and it will be a rich golden brown. Remember to keep the water topped up during cooking, especially on Christmas morning when there are lots of other things on your mind.

8 oz (225 g) self-raising flour
1 level teaspoon (5 ml) mixed spice
½ level teaspoon grated nutmeg
1 level teaspoon (5 ml) salt
12 oz (325 g) currants
12 oz (325 g) sultanas
12 oz (325 g) stoned raisins
12 oz (325 g) fresh white breadcrumbs
12 oz (325 g) suet, finely chopped
4 oz (100 g) candied peel, finely chopped
2 oz (50 g) almonds, blanched and chopped
1 cooking apple, peeled, cored and grated
Grated rind and juice of 1 orange
1 lb (450 g) soft brown sugar
6 eggs, beaten
¼ pint (150 ml) extra-dry cider such as Bulmers Number 7

Grease two 2½-pint pudding basins.

Sift together the flour, mixed spice, nutmeg and salt.

Put the dried fruit into a bowl with the breadcrumbs, suet, peel, almonds, grated apple, orange rind and juice. Stir in the spiced flour and sugar. Finally add the eggs and cider. Stir the mixture well, then turn into the basins.

Cover the tops with greaseproof paper and a foil lid and let the puddings simmer gently for about 7 hours. Lift them out of the pan, leaving the foil and greaseproof paper in place. Cool and store the puddings.

Simmer for a further 3 hours before serving.

Herefordshire Cider Cake

A spicy cake that the family will love.

1 orange
Sweet cider such as Woodpecker
4 oz (100 g) margarine
6 oz (175 g) caster sugar
2 eggs
8 oz (225 g) self-raising flour
½ level teaspoon mixed spice
½ level teaspoon cinnamon
8 oz (220 g) currants

Heat the oven to 350°F (180°C), Mark 4. Line and grease the base and sides of a 7-inch cake tin.

Grate the rind from the orange and squeeze out the juice. Make juice up to ¼ pint with cider.

Cream the margarine and sugar in a bowl with the orange rind until light and fluffy. Beat in the eggs one at a time.

Sift the flour and spices together. Stir into the mixture with the currants and cider until mixed to a dropping consistency.

Turn into the tin, smooth the top and bake in the oven for about 1 hour or until the cake feels firm to the touch and a warmed skewer inserted in the centre comes out clean. Leave cake to cool in the tin for about 10 minutes before turning it out. Remove the paper and leave to finish cooling on a wire rack.

Cider for Drinking

Good cider 'tis a drink divine,
Better by far than all your wine,
Good in grief, good in joy,
Good for maid, man and boy. ANON 19th century

A country pub, a rustic bench and tankards of fine draught cider, the amber liquid sparkling in the early evening sun. Throw in a spreading chestnut tree and a couple of West Country yeomen and, for most people, the traditional picture of cider drinking is complete. "Cider is wonderfully refreshing on hot days and for restoring energy when you're tired, but it should never be drunk at any other time" is the advice given by writers of some years ago. Clearly, they have never tried the connoisseur's cider Bulmers Number 7, or shared the dinner table with Bulmers Special Cellar which is one of the finest accompaniments to poultry dishes ever produced.

The truth is that, whatever the occasion or time of day, there is a blend of cider to suit. Traditional draught cider, sold only in public houses, is still the magnificent drink it ever was but it is not the only cider available.

Today, more than ever, cider is sold to be drunk in the home. For indoors and outdoors, Strongbow, rich, full-bodied, a man's drink, rivals the sweeter sparkling Woodpecker in popularity. Yet Dry Woodpecker, with its subtle taste, is equally valuable on convivial occasions, appealing to the sophisticated palate.

Different ciders such as Dry Reserve and Special Cellar are worth looking out for, especially as not all blends of cider are generally available. Dry Reserve is a truly praiseworthy cider for those who like a full-bodied, richly coloured drink with a light sparkle. Special Cellar is slightly sweeter and not sparkling. Sold in attractive flasks, it enhances the appearance of the dinner table as well as the appetite of the guests. Both these ciders make excellent aperitifs, sharpening the palate and heightening appreciation of the meal to come.

Finally, there is the aristocrat of all ciders, Pomagne. It is available sweet or dry and is just the choice for parties, its bubbling effervescence having all the gaiety of champagne at a fraction of the price.

Cider, incidentally, can be drunk out of any type of glass, although the fruity, full-bodied brands are more at home in tankards. Good cider, however, deserves beautiful glassware and this was the belief of the seventeenth- and eighteenth-century cider drinkers. Some special cider glasses made of English lead crystal in the eighteenth century still exist. The shape has no special significance, but the glasses are hand engraved with the most exquisite reproductions of apple branches and the codlin moth, the beautiful pest of the orchard.

The 1st Viscount Scudamore, who laid the foundations of the modern cider industry, had a special set of cider glasses made. Each glass stood 14½ inches high, had feet 5 inches in diameter and held more than a pint of Lord Scudamore's precious cider. Only one of the original set survives and is in the London Museum, but modern reproductions have been produced by Webb Corbett, a fitting tribute to cider's growing importance today.

Chairman's Special

for about twelve

This really is a chairman's special created by Bertram Bulmer of Bulmers Cider. He insists that only the bright yellow thinly cut peel of the lemon is used, as the inclusion of any white pithy peel would make the drink bitter. It is essential to serve really cold.

2 bottles Dry Pomagne
2 bottles dry white wine
Thinly cut lemon peel
2 wine glasses sherry
2 wine glasses brandy
6 oz (175 g) raspberries
2 bananas

Chill the Pomagne and wine.

Place the lemon peel in a very large jug or bowl with the sherry for half an hour before use. Add the Pomagne, wine and brandy with the raspberries and thinly sliced bananas.

Pomagne Cocktail

This cocktail is best made by the glassful rather than mixing in a jug as there are few ingredients. Only use the outside yellow zest of the lemon.

Brandy
Pomagne
Lemon twists

Place two tablespoons of brandy in the bottom of a white wine glass. Top up with well-chilled Dry Pomagne and place a twist of lemon in each glass.

Midsummer Fruit Cup

makes eight to ten glasses

A refreshing fruity drink that everybody will love.

2 tablespoons (30 ml) honey
1 pint (600 ml) cold water
2 lemons
¾ pint (450 ml) dry cider such as Strongbow
4 oz (100 g) picked strawberries
Broken ice

Put the honey with ¼ pint (150 ml) water in a small pan and heat until the honey has dissolved. Leave to cool.

Thinly slice one lemon and place in a large jug with the juice from the other lemon. Add the remaining ¾ pint (450 ml) cold water, the honey water and the cider. Mix well.

Chill well and just before serving stir in the strawberries and a little broken ice.

Henley Special

makes six glasses

A perfect drink for those who enjoy a long, non-alcoholic drink.

1 bottle Apple Juice
1 split bottle dry ginger
12 ice cubes
6 small sprigs of mint

Thoroughly chill the Apple Juice and ginger.

Pour into a jug and mix well, then add the ice cubes. Pour into 6 tall glasses and float a sprig of mint on top of each drink.

Iced Grapefruit

makes ten glasses

Try this on a really hot day when very thirsty and serve very, very cold.

4 tablespoons (60 ml) concentrated unsweetened grapefruit juice
1 flagon (38 fl oz, 1 litre) dry cider such as Strongbow
Sprigs of mint

Thoroughly chill the grapefruit and cider.

Place in a large jug, mix well together and pour into glasses. Top each with a sprig of mint.

Fresh Summer Sparkler

makes six glasses

For a more special drink add cubes of iced melon to the drink.

1 pint (600 ml) can unsweetened orange juice
1 pint (600 ml) dry cider such as Dry Reserve
A few slices cucumber

Thoroughly chill the orange juice and cider.

Turn into a large jug and mix well. Add the slices of cucumber and pour into glasses.

Summer Celebration Cup

makes six to ten glasses

A delicious drink to serve on a hot day.

8 oz (225 g) small strawberries
3 tablespoons (45 ml) orange liqueur
1 orange
1 pint (600 ml) medium-dry cider such as Dry Woodpecker
1 pint (600 ml) soda water
Ice

Wash and hull the strawberries and place in a small bowl. Add the orange liqueur and the juice of the orange. Cover and leave to stand in a cool place overnight.

Next day add the cider, soda water and ice cubes. Serve in glasses.

Hereford Redstreak

makes six glasses

Redstreak is one of the earliest and finest Herefordshire cider apples. Hence the name of this drink.

1 bottle Dry Reserve, chilled
Thinly peeled rind of 1 lemon
1 wine glass gin

Make sure the cider is put to chill. Place the lemon rind in a large jug, pour over the gin and leave to stand for 30 minutes.

When the guests arrive pour on the cider and serve at once.

All Seasons Fruit Cup

makes eight glasses

This is my favourite drink of them all. If there is a hint of sunshine and we are entertaining a crowd at Sunday lunchtime it always seems popular.

Two ½ pint (300 ml) tonics
Two 9½ oz (300 ml) bottles of Bulmers Number 7
6¼ oz (175 g) carton frozen concentrated orange juice,
    thawed
12 ice cubes
Sprigs of mint
Orange slices

Chill the tonics and the cider.

Make the orange juice up to 1 pint (600 ml) with cold water and add the tonics, cider and ice cubes. Mix well and serve in glasses decorated with sprigs of mint and orange slices.

From left to right:
All Seasons Fruit Cup, Sangria, Blackcurrant Cooler

Sangria

makes sixteen glasses

An easy party drink, great for holiday parties.

2 lemons, sliced
2 oranges, sliced
2 apples, cored and sliced
12 ice cubes
4 pints (2 litres) sweet cider such as Special Cellar
2 bottles inexpensive red wine
1 glass brandy
2 to 4 tablespoons (30 to 60 ml) caster sugar (to taste)

Chill the cider and wine well.

Place all the ingredients together in a very large mixing bowl and stir thoroughly. Serve at once in wine glasses.

Blackcurrant Cooler

for one

A great favourite with everybody. Make up the whole flagon for a crowd and watch it disappear.

¼ pint (150 ml) sweet cider such as Woodpecker, chilled
1 tablespoon (15 ml) blackcurrant drink

Pour the cider into a glass and stir in the blackcurrant. Serve at once.

Glühwein

makes ten glasses

A lovely hot punch to serve on cold winter's evenings.

2 lemons
1 bottle inexpensive red wine
1 pint (600 ml) Apple Juice
8 cloves
1 stick cinnamon
2 to 4 oz (50 to 100 g) caster sugar
A sherry glass of brandy (optional)

Peel the zest very thinly from the lemons, cut a few slices of lemon for the garnish. Squeeze the remaining lemons to extract the juice.

Put the lemon zest, juice, wine, Apple Juice, cloves and cinnamon into a pan. Cover and bring to just below simmering point and leave it at this temperature for 1 hour or more. Lift out the lemon rind, cloves and cinnamon. Add sugar to taste.

Serve hot with lemon slices floating on top. Add the brandy just before serving if a more potent drink is favoured.

Champion's Cup

makes twelve glasses

A mixture of wine and Pomagne is a subtle refreshing drink. Vary this drink to your own taste. If you like a sweeter drink use a sweeter white wine and a sweet Pomagne. If you are not sure, try mixing the two.

1 bottle dry white wine
1 bottle Pomagne

Thoroughly chill the Pomagne and wine. Blend the two together just before serving.

Orange Quencher

makes six to eight glasses

Essential that this is served really cold; it is delightfully refreshing at any time of year. I serve it as an aperitif.

1 bottle Pomagne
6¼ oz (175 g) carton frozen concentrated orange juice,
    thawed

Chill the Pomagne.

Make the orange juice up to 1 pint (600 ml) with cold water. Mix with the Pomagne just before serving.